GOD Needs To Hear Thank YOU, Too!

A FATHER'S
LIGHT AND LESSONS
FOR MY CHILDREN

IRA KNIGHT

Published by Freed Slave Publishing

P.O. Box 51475

Durham, North Carolina 27717

Copyright © 2005 by Ira Knight

Second edition © 2014 by Ira Knight

Printed in the United States of America

ISBN: 0977415600

INTRODUCTION

This book is offered as a tool, mirror and bridge – a gift of inspiration to ourselves.

Too often in life we spend a great deal of time and energy looking at and dwelling on the things we lack, instead of looking at the blessings and things we do have.

****

I Thank YOU GOD for everything.

I thank Jimmie Greene, for being a true Man and reflection of GOD.

****

If you any feedback, comments to share, or interested in Ira Knight visiting your book club, community, organization or other event, you can contact him via:

Email: Ira_Knight@yahoo.com

Website: www.IraKnight.org

CONTENTS

MANHOOD

"When I was a child, I talked like a child,
understood as a child, I reasoned like a child, but
when I became a man, I put away childish things."

(1 Corinthians 13:11)

A PARENT'S BLESSING

Thank YOU GOD for blessing me with the privilege to be a parent and father.
Thank YOU for YOUR wisdom, guidance and understanding.
Thank YOU for blessing me to live the life YOU created me to live.

Thank you for blessing my children to witness me living this life of purpose.

Thank YOU for Blessing me to understand that:

A.

It is my responsibility to:

1. Pay attention
2. Look for the good
3. Guide and teach them to seek and understand YOU.
4. Prepare them for the day when i am no longer here, to know that they always have YOU.
5. Prepare them to love, live and enjoy their lives ... it is a gift from YOU.
6. Understand that YOU have already placed YOUR Light in them.

B.

1. My children are <u>not</u> my property.
2. i am not here to live my unfulfilled life, visions and dreams through my children, but to help and witness them living the lives YOU purposed for them.
3. It is not my job, role or right to crush or subject their will to mine.
4. They are part of YOUR PLAN and PURPOSE.
5. i am blessed for having children come through me.

C.

I am responsible for:
1. Observing,
2. Recognizing
3. Nurturing
4. Encouraging
5. Developing the talents, gifts and abilities that YOU sent my children to this earth with.

DEATH

Thank you GOD for death.

Not as something to fear or desire or chase, but as something to understand.

To understand that death has a place in YOUR PLAN.

That death is not the end, but a continuation...

A step closer to YOU

death helps me:

to understand that my time here is limited.

death helps me to appreciate:

the gift of time

the gift of good people

the gift of relationships

death intensifies my sense of urgency -- i know my time is limited, not limitless.

SURVIVAL

i Thank YOU GOD that i have survived.

i Thank YOU for the days when i woke up every morning, and hated to get out of bed.
Hated the day i had to face.
Hated going to work at a job i hated doing.
Making more money than i had ever made.
My employers did me no wrong in allowing me to do this to myself.

i couldn't wait to get home so i could kill the day and die.
Just so i could get ready to do it again tomorrow.

i took awhile before i realized i was committing suicide.
i wasn't using a gun or sleeping pills or poison or a noose.
It was nice and clean and respectable.
Nothing sudden or unexpected.
i was doing it gradually...slowly... over 10, 20, 30 even 40 years.

i was letting my life force leak out – 1 day at a time.

i Thank YOU that YOU answered when i begged for mercy and deliverance.

When i asked,
"Why did YOU allow this to happen to me?"

SURVIVAL (cont'd)

YOU answered
"How did i allow this to happen to myself?"

YOU asked me
 "Why was i wasting the precious gifts given to me?
The gifts of Time. A Brain. A Mind. Energy. Life.
Another Day."
YOU told me to check my inventory.
YOU made it clear that what YOU made a part of me
that no one could take away.
i could not use it and let it go to waste...
To remember that no one in the universe has the power
or authority to take it from me.

They are gifts from YOU.

A LOVER'S APOLOGY

June 21, ___

A,

Unfortunately the people i can hurt the most are the ones closest to me.

Often times i brood a lot because i know once the words leave my lips i cannot make them come back.

Tonight i said words and expressed an attitude that hurt you. With anyone else and people who mean nothing to me in the scheme of things, i would have been more diplomatic. But with you i took liberties and for granted that i could be "candid" in a manner that makes no sense at all. I can't say i'm sorry because those two words are absolutely inadequate.
This has made me realize that i focused on what you are not and what you didn't do rather than what you are and what you do. Improperly honing in on your weakness rather than your strengths. What i lost sight of is how we complement each other – in my weaknesses you are strong, and in your weakness i provide strength. I see that balance reflected in SIK daily.
I realize that i've been the thoughtless one when i recall that the best celebration i ever had as an adult, was when you returned from Mexico with the beautiful chess sets ... and candlelight dinner.

A LOVER'S APOLOGY (cont'd)

As i travel back i remember your humble attitude when you chased me down on campus to apologize when you thought you had been rude to me. I remember going to K___ where you ate and we talked...

I remember the first Sunday i visited you at your parent's house – your family had already completed dinner, but you were humble enough to cook for me – banana pancakes with no syrup – with gratitude and <u>no</u> attitude.

I think about driving to S___ with a busted window covered with a plastic bag.

I think about driving 17 hours from N___ to S__.

I think about how you put that beautiful gold link bracelet on layaway and presented it for christmas.

I reflect on where i was at those stages of my life and where you were and i know and understand that i was blessed that you chose me.

I say and bring up these things as a reminder to me of how good you have been to me and for me.

I have not forgotten that before i met you, i thought fine dining was NCl___.

I say this because although i've grown and in many ways, the old me is unrecognizable, the good things and good people – especially you – that have been important and are important help to keep me grounded.

A LOVER'S APOLOGY (cont'd)

I will put my best efforts into delivering the respect, honor and credit that is yours.

I sincerely Apologize, However, i do not want you to accept it right away simply because "that is what you are supposed to do when someone apologizes". I need you to reflect and think about it. Let me know after you've done that.

AMERICAN SLAVERY

i thank YOU GOD for American Slavery.
Not biblical slavery.
Not hebrew slavery.
Not egyptian slavery.
But American Slavery.

i thank YOU because it forced me to find out who
YOU are.
It forced me to find out who i am.
The pain got my attention.
The pain peeled my eyes open.
The pain focused my mind.
The pain raised questions that had to be
answered.
The pain removed fear.

American Slavery has taught me:

the truth of YOUR Law of "Cause and Effect".
Conscious deeds and behavior reveal true belief,
faith and motives...
Beautiful language, eloquent, forceful, pleasing and
convincing words, confessions and declarations of
faith mean nothing compared to actions and
deeds.

<u>American Slavery has shown me:</u>
the GOD in man.
the Devil in man.
How segregation and racism in America did not rise from a void, but evolved from American Slavery.
How brown, tan, caramel and other skin shades became 'black' as identifiers.
That i have no desire or taste for revenge or repayment – actions and philosophies so heinous – only YOU can balance this.

<u>American Slavery has ensured that i will not be extorted or exploited by fear or ignorance:</u>

How much worse than American Slavery can any <u>other</u> hell possibly be?
What pain, suffering and torment could be worse than that of an enslaved father?

AMERICAN SLAVERY (cont'd)

American Slavery has made clear the value and impact of a father:

The results of standard, routine, systematic and accepted violation of the **sacred** parent-child relationship.

A father powerless to protect his mate and children from the common torture, abuse and imprisonment of spirit and soul killers.

A father that could not nurture and develop his children into the man or woman YOU created them to be.

A father who could not teach his children to utilize YOUR gifts to be the best they could be, to improve their own lives, for their self-benefit.

Children learning there were no honest, just and proper rewards for hard, honest work or ingenious ideas. No just incentives.

A father with no voice in teaching his children to be what YOU created them to be.

A father whose children cannot aspire to be what he is.

A father that has to teach his children mortal fear in order to spare their lives.

A father whose children cannot look up to him as a child would.

A father with a future of absolute uncertainty.

A father whose only certainty is death.

A father who has to witness and endure crushed potential as a 'normal' and accepted way of life.

A father subject to the will of a fellow man.

A father with no rights as a family man.

A father with no <u>visible</u> hope.

AMERICAN SLAVERY (cont'd)

American Slavery has revealed possibilities:

In the midst of this American Slavery, YOU raised up one of the greatest men to ever walk this planet Earth.
A possibility model of what YOU created man to be in Frederick Douglass.

A possibility model.
Not a role model.
Not a symbol.
Not an icon.
A true and living example of what can be accomplished when man seeks and worships YOU in spirit and in truth.

American Slavery has sown seeds of Inspiration:

If Frederick Douglass can make his mark in YOUR world, from his beginning, condition and circumstances, there is nothing i cannot do.

Thank YOU for giving Frederick Douglass his book, "My Bondage and My Freedom".

American Slavery has provided a Clear Mind and Brain:

i thank YOU that American Slavery has brought me to know YOU with a certainty that no man, books or tradition can shake.

"As iron sharpens iron, so one man sharpens another."

(Proverbs 27:17)

"To everything there is a season, and a time to every purpose..."

(Ecclesiastes 3:1)

FAILURE

i thank YOU GOD for failure.

i thank YOU for this great teacher, because it has taught me:

to recognize YOU.

who and what i am not.

To be honest and true with myself.
To continuously evaluate my hunger and desires.
How strong YOU have made me.
How merciful YOU have been to me.
Understanding and patience.
To understand and value setbacks.
To understand time and timing.

To realize with every effort, that this is not my last chance, but my next chance.
That as long as i am alive i have hope and a chance.

To be content but not complacent.

To discern truth and untruth.
To love life.

To know what i have learned from YOU.
To face life without fear.
To LOVE LIFE.
To become a source of inspiration and not envy.

RESPECT

i come before YOU with all the respect and awe YOU inspire.
i come knowing that i am in the presence of the Lord and Creator of all worlds and universes.
i come knowing that YOU imagined, designed, created, placed and set in motion the planets, stars and all other celestial bodies.
i come knowing that YOU established principles that we uncover as natural, scientific, physical and spiritual laws.
i understand the more i learn about YOUR established principles, the more i learn about YOU.

i thank YOU GOD for making it clear to me:

that when i respect YOU i respect YOUR creation... YOUR creatures.

That i cannot respect YOU and deliberately abuse and mistreat YOUR creatures or ignore the suffering of... YOUR woman, YOUR man.

i cannot mislead, abuse and exploit YOUR man and woman and sincerely respect or honor YOU.

When i respect YOU, i understand that YOU are THE SOURCE, THE ORIGINATOR, THE NOURISHER and PROVIDER, therefore there is no shortage of resources

RESPECT (cont'd)

There is no need for me to harm or deprive my fellow creation to enjoy what YOU have for me.

i respect that YOU are not just a wish & desire granter, living in outer space – waiting to serve me – but THE LORD of every world and every universe – with a PLAN and a PURPOSE.

i respect that YOUR PLAN succeeds, YOUR WILL is done, YOUR PURPOSE achieved – whether i willingly submit to it or not.

i respect that YOU can be revealed but not imprisoned in a book.

i understand that proper respect and awe of YOU is the beginning of knowledge.

i acknowledge that we are not peers and i understand and respect this about our relationship.

i understand that YOU have created each and every human being with talents, gifts and abilities.

i understand that YOU have created each one of us to have a fulfilling role in YOUR PLAN.

As i have realized and acted on this knowledge i have had peace and a peaceful life.

i cannot fully grasp and understand YOUR PLAN, but it has been simple to understand YOU and YOUR WAYS.

FORGIVENESS

Thank YOU GOD for forgiving me of my sins and transgressions, misdeeds and wrongdoings.

i Thank YOU for forgiving me for the damage, harm, bad examples, ill feelings, bad experiences and stumbling blocks that i've caused to others.

Thank YOU for blessing me to forgive those who have sinned against me, done ill and wrong to me.

i Thank YOU for this Freedom.
i Thank YOU for the freedom from bearing and carrying the weight of grudges, anger and resentment that YOU did not design and create me to carry.

EVERYDAY BLESSINGS

"Try looking for the good, you'll find it."

"Every day we wake up is another chance to work at making our visions and dreams a reality."

MIRACLES

Thank YOU GOD that YOU are still in the miracle business every single day.

i thank YOU that i woke up today.

i thank YOU that i was the one of countless millions that left my father and survived to cling to my mother's wall, evolve and enter this world.

i acknowledge that this happens everyday.

i thank YOU that i do not have to remember to:

Breathe when i'm asleep or when i'm awake.
Remind my heart to beat.
Put one foot in front of the other to walk and run.

> i thank YOU for the miraculous brain, mind and imagination that YOU've placed in every man and woman.

i thank YOU that:

i lift a switch and there is light in my home.
i slide a switch and there is heat and cool air in my home.
i turn a knob and there is warm water for my body.

MIRACLES (cont'd)

i press a button and i have access to words, ideas, activities and events from all over this planet Earth.

i pick up a piece of plastic and metal, press buttons and i hear voices from all over the planet Earth.

i click buttons and send and receive words and ideas all over the planet Earth.

i press a button that says "on" and i hear sounds, music, voices and inspiration as often as i choose.

i put the key in my car, turn it, and go anywhere i want to go with no understanding of how it miraculously all works.

i go to the grocery store to buy milk and eggs and i drink and eat them without a second thought about what it takes for them to get here.

i get in an airplane and take trips to places which once took months and years to travel to.
i ride above the clouds, at a comfortable temperature and rarely give it a second thought.

i thank YOU, again, for the miraculous brain, mind and imagination that YOU've placed in every man and woman.

GOOD PEOPLE

Thank YOU for the Good People ... YOUR People.
These people that i know are YOUR People by their
actions, behavior, conscious deeds and spirit ...
NOT by their confessions or professions of faith.

Thank YOU:

For friends that are more than family when i had only
relatives.

For the grandmothers, aunts, uncles, grandfathers when
we had none.

For the people who literally fed me when i was hungry
and had no food to eat.

For the people who literally housed me when i was
homeless and had nowhere to go.

Thank YOU for:

YOUR People at the church, at the masjid and in the
street.
YOUR People as clerks at hotels and movie theaters.
YOUR People as cashiers and clerks at fast food
restaurants.

<u>GOOD PEOPLE (cont'd)</u>

YOUR People that could not read but were able to teach me so much about YOU.

i Thank YOU for showing me YOUR People by their deeds and spirit.

Thank YOU for blessing me with eyes to penetrate creeds, customs, confessions and declarations of faith.

i Thank YOU that i can see YOU in Good People.

MERCY

Thank YOU that YOU are GOD, LORD, Creator and Nourisher of all worlds and universes.

Thank YOU that YOU are GOD, not a man to think & behave like vicious men and women.

That YOU have made it clear that i was created by YOU, not that YOU were created by me.

> Thank YOU that YOU are not vicious & brutal as men that YOU would let such a brief trial period of this life experience sentence me to an eternity of misery in a hell or a heaven.

Thank YOU that heaven is not streets paved with gold, pearly gates, the most delicious and exquisite foods all day & all night – anyone that can accumulate enough wealth can have that right here.

Thank YOU that hell is not a life of never ending pain, torment, misery, lack & deprivation – that was the daily life of an american slave during American Slavery. That is also the life of the poverty stricken in New York, North Carolina, North and South America, Africa, Australia, Europe & Asia.

Thank YOU that hell is not an eternity completely removed from YOUR presence, since YOU are OMNIPRESENT.

FAMILY & FRIENDS

"A friend loves at all times, and a brother is born
for adversity."

(Proverbs 17:17)

A MOTHER & A SECOND CHANCE

Thank YOU GOD for my Mother and a second chance.
Thank YOU GOD for the second chance to tell my
mother while she is alive.

> Thank you for blessing me with the name you
> blessed me with -- there is no way you could
> fully understand and comprehend this name.

> Thank you for never abandoning us, even as
> rough and crucial as times and situations
> were. i can really understand it now.

> When i was upset about your silence and
> unwillingness to to explain matters to me, i
> thank you for not burdening me with adult
> matters before i was prepared, equipped and
> able to handle them.

Thank you for never bad mouthing my sperm donor and
allowing me to observe and learn the truth about his
character for myself.

Thank you for checking me the first and only time you
heard me use profanity in your presence.

Thank you for buying all of the city's newspapers for me
to read daily.

Thank you for the encyclopedias – to teach me to
research and find information.
As expensive as it was, thank you for living at the
calming ocean view of 2403.

Thank you for giving me space to crawl, walk, run, jump and fly.

AUNT D____

Dear Aunt D__,

I know that we have not always seen eye to eye over the years.

But in reflecting back on my life, the lives of my brothers and experiencing and observing my children – certain things come to mind.

I constantly think about the pitfalls and hardships each of my brothers have had to deal with. I always wondered how I managed to avoid many of their issues. We all lived with my mother and grew up in the same household.

The one factor that stands out every time is, I was the only one to leave New York to live and go to school in North Carolina. The more I think about it the more I realize that this was a key that has made all the difference. I had a chance to see and live another life other than what we experienced in Brooklyn.

Now that I have lived as an adult without children and with children of my own, I can begin to understand the significant lifestyle change you made—the sacrifices you made to give up freedoms you were accustomed to, comforts you were used to – to become a full-time parent for 2 years. Packing lunch every day, preparing dinner every day, homework and projects every day, washing and ironing clothes, etc.

AUNT D____(cont'd)

However, the most incredible and enduring memory I have is from the fall of 19__. I had a class project to collect leaves – I tell

A____ about this and I'll tell my children, because I remember it as if it happened yesterday:

> We went out in wet, dark and miserable weather to that church on Panola Street to get a magnolia leaf. We then drove out to the country, pulling into that woman's yard, you getting out of the car, knocking on the door and asking the woman if you could get leaves from her "weeping willow" tree.

> As long as I live, I know I will never forget that day – I smile and shake my head in amazement every time I think about it.

I just had to write and share this with you for 2 reasons:

1. The more I look at my brothers and my children the more significant and valuable those experiences become.
2. I thank GOD that I have the chance and ability to do so.

Thanks again.

September 10, ___

KKW,

This is just a short note to thank you for the fellowship.
I can't express how great it was to see you both this
past weekend. It's difficult to express exactly how much
it meant that you thought enough of us, that it was an
important priority for you to "track us down" for a visit.

I know that it's been way too many years since we've
seen each other. I know personally as we go through
life's challenges and struggles, sometimes we withdraw,
not realizing that although it's about us, but not <u>all</u>
about us. That we are important to other people.

Even through putting words on paper, I can't adequately
express what a blessing for all of us to get together,
eat, hang out and talk. It was quite an inspiration.

Thanks again.

With Love from
i

About the Author

Ira Knight understands the gift of inspiration and the power of encouragement. For him it's not rumor or hearsay, it's a way of life. To this end, all of his work is created with the spirit and intent of making the world a better place than the one he entered.

Books:

THE Man's Guide To Writing Love Letters
GOD Needs To Hear Thank YOU, Too!
I'm Teaching Poetry, Volume 1

Plays:

1 Life 2 Live
When Ralph Waldo Emerson Met The Frederick Douglass
Who Shall Speak For the Defense?!
It's Spring Again

Workshops:

Ira has conducted workshops, group and individual, on topics including writing, the creation process, producing, publishing and manifesting ideas.

If you are interested in Ira Knight visiting your book club, community, church, organization or as a participant in your event, you can contact him via:

Email: Ira_Knight@yahoo.com
Website: www.IraKnight.org